Alaska

by Patricia K. Kummer,
Capstone Press
Geography Department

Content Consultant
Nancy Ferrell
Alaska resident and author of *Alaska: A Land in Motion*

C A P S T O N E
H I G H / L O W B O O K S
an imprint of Capstone Press

8815183

CAPSTONE PRESS

818 North Willow Street • Mankato, MN 56001
http://www.capstone-press.com

Library of Congress Cataloging-in-Publication Data
Kummer, Patricia K.
    Alaska/by Patricia K. Kummer.
        p.cm.--(One nation)
    Includes bibliographical references and index.
    Summary: An overview of the state of Alaska, including its history, geography, people, and living conditions.
        ISBN 1-56065-679-4
        1. Alaska--Juvenile literature. [1.Alaska.] I. Title. II. Series.
F904.3.K86 1998
979.8--dc21

                                    97-40817
                                       CIP
                                        AC

Editorial Credits: Editor, Cara Van Voorst; cover design and illustrations, Timothy Halldin; photo research, Michelle L. Norstad

Photo Credits:
Alaska Division of Tourism, 4, 6, 16, 37
Michelle Burgess, 33
Dembinsky Photo Assoc., 40
William B. Folsom, 9
Helen Longest-Slaughter, 23
Dan Polin, 12, 28
Root Resources/Kitty Kohout, 5; Bill Christensen, 47
Lynn Sheldon Jr., 10
Unicorn Stock Photos/Jean Higgins, 20
Visuals Unlimited/Steve McCutcheon, 5, 16; Charles Rushing, 25, 30; Jeff Greenberg, 34
Wild Things, cover

Table of Contents

Fast Facts about Alaska

State Flag

Location: At the northwestern tip of North America, between the Arctic and Pacific Oceans

Size: 586,424 square miles (1,524,702 square kilometers)

Population: 603,617 (1996 U.S. Census Bureau estimate)

Capital: Juneau

Date admitted to the Union: January 3, 1959; the 49th state

Willow ptarmigan

Forget-me-not

Largest cities: Anchorage, Fairbanks, Juneau, Sitka, Ketchikan, Kodiak, Kenai, Bethel, Valdez, Wasilla

Nicknames: Last Frontier, Land of the Midnight Sun

State bird: Willow ptarmigan

State flower: Forget-me-not

State tree: Sitka spruce

State song: "Alaska's Flag," by Marie Drake and Elinor Dusenbury

Sitka spruce

Chapter 1

The Iditarod

The Iditarod Trail Sled Dog Race covers 1,161 miles (1,868 kilometers) in Alaska. Alaskans call the Iditarod the Last Great Race on Earth.

The race starts in Anchorage on the first Saturday of March. It ends in Nome about 10 to 21 days later. The first musher who reaches Nome wins $50,000 and a new truck. A musher is the driver of a sled-dog team.

Mushers and their sled dogs must withstand cold weather during the Iditarod. They cross frozen land and rivers during the Iditarod. They race through the Alaska and Kuskokwim Ranges.

The Iditarod Trail
In the early 1900s, people mainly used the first Iditarod trail as a mail route. It ran from Knik to Nome. The present-day race trail runs from Anchorage to Nome.

Mushers and their sled dogs cross frozen land during the Iditarod.

The first Iditarod occurred in 1973. It honored mushers of 1925. In that year, sled dog teams followed part of the Iditarod Trail.

The sled dog teams carried medicine that prevented a diphtheria epidemic. Diptheria is a deadly illness that attacks the heart and nervous system. An epidemic is the rapid spread of an illness through a population.

Sled Dog Teams

Sled dog teams were once Alaska's major form of transportation. Transportation is the system and means of moving people and goods. Snowmobiles and airplanes have now replaced sled dogs.

Today, people use sled dog teams mostly for racing. Alaska hosts several shorter sled dog races in addition to the Iditarod.

Some Alaskans still use dog sleds in the bush. The bush is wilderness areas with few roads. These Alaskans mush to get from one place to another. Mush means to travel using a sled dog team. Sometimes they mush into villages to get supplies.

Other Transportation

Alaska has only a few major highways. People often must fly in planes and use boats to travel.

Today, mushing is mainly a sport.

Some Alaskan villages are only reachable by small planes. Bush pilots fly supplies and people into and out of these villages.

People in southern Alaska use the Alaska Marine Highway. This is a system of ferries. A ferry is a boat that carries people and automobiles. These boats travel from Skagway and Ketchikan to Bellingham, Washington. Other ferries connect the Kenai Peninsula, Kodiak Island, and the Aleutian Islands.

Chapter 2
The Land

Alaska is the nation's largest state. It sits at the far northwestern tip of North America. Northern Alaska touches the Arctic Ocean. The Gulf of Alaska and the North Pacific Ocean border southern and southeastern Alaska. Canada borders Alaska to the east. The Bering Sea and the Chukchi Sea separate western Alaska from Russia.

Land of the Midnight Sun

Northern Alaska has many days when the sun does not set. The town of Barrow has continual daylight from May 10 to August 2. This happens because Alaska is close to the North Pole. The North Pole is closest to the sun during the summer.

Barrow also has days when the sun does not rise. People in Barrow live in darkness from November 18 to January 24.

The Gulf of Alaska borders southern and southeastern Alaska.

Mount McKinley's peak is the highest point in North America.

Coastline and Islands

Alaska has the longest coastline of all the states. The coastline is 6,640 miles (10,690 kilometers) long. Alaska's lowest point is along its coast. The coast is at sea level. Sea level is the average level of the ocean's surface.

More than 1,800 islands lie along Alaska's coast. The largest is Kodiak Island. Kodiak Island is east of the Alaska Peninsula in the Gulf of Alaska. The Aleutian Islands is a long chain of islands. It lies between the Bering Sea and the North Pacific Ocean.

Alaska's Mountains

The Brooks Range stretches across northern Alaska. This range is the northern part of the Rocky Mountains.

The Pacific Mountain System curves across southern Alaska. It includes the Alaska, Wrangell, Saint Elias, and Coastal Ranges. Sixteen of the nation's highest peaks rise among these ranges. The Alaska and Wrangell Ranges have about 80 active volcanoes.

Mount McKinley's peak is the highest point in North America. This peak is 20,320 feet (6,096 meters) above sea level. Mount McKinley stands in the Alaska Range.

The Coastal and Saint Elias Ranges rise along southeastern Alaska. Glaciers lie at the foot of these mountains. A glacier is a huge sheet of slowly moving ice. Malaspina Glacier is Alaska's largest glacier. It lies at the foot of Mount St. Elias.

The Central Uplands and Lowlands

The Central Uplands and Lowlands lie between Alaska's mountain systems. Low mountains and rolling hills form the uplands. Muskeg covers the lowlands. Muskeg is soft, wet land.

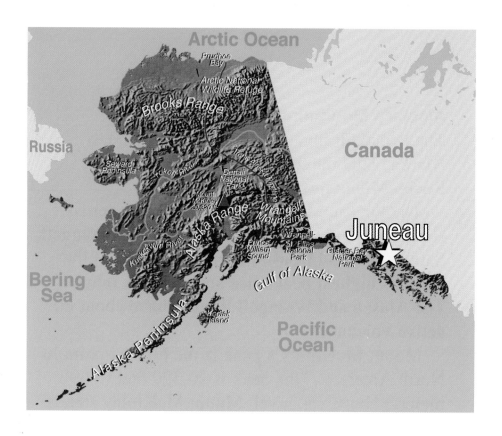

The Yukon River is the third-longest river in the United States. Both the Kuskokwim and Yukon Rivers flow west through central Alaska. These rivers carry water from the Central Uplands and Lowlands to the Bering Sea.

The Arctic Coastal Plain

The Arctic Coastal Plain lies along the Arctic Ocean. Land on the plain is called tundra. Tundra is treeless land where the ground below surface level is always frozen.

The surface of the tundra thaws in the summer. Then colorful wildflowers and short grasses grow on the tundra.

Wildlife

Black bears, brown bears, and polar bears live in Alaska. Dall sheep climb the state's mountains. Caribou live in Alaska's wilderness areas.

Seals, otters, and whales swim along Alaska's coast. Salmon and halibut also swim along the coast. Puffins nest near the shores. Bald eagles fly above Alaska.

Climate

Alaska's climate varies from region to region because of its size. Summers are hot and winters are cold in the middle of the state. The record summer temperature at Fort Yukon is 100 degrees Fahrenheit (56 degrees Centigrade). Winter temperatures reach minus 80 degrees Fahrenheit (minus 44 degrees Centigrade).

Parts of southeastern Alaska receive up to 200 inches of rain and snow each year. Northern Alaskans live in darkness throughout the winter. They live in 24-hour daylight during part of the short, cool summer.

Chapter 3

The People

Alaska has the third-smallest population among the states despite its size. There is enough room for each Alaskan to have one square mile (2.6 kilometers) of land. However, 67 percent of Alaskans live in or near cities.

Anchorage and Fairbanks have the state's largest populations. Many Alaskans also live in Juneau, Sitka, and Ketchikan.

Population Growth

Alaska is one of the fastest-growing states in the nation. Between 1990 and 1995, its population increased by nearly 10 percent.

Only one-third of today's Alaskans were born in the state. The other two-thirds are from other states and countries. Early settlers worked in Alaska's whaling, fishing, mining, and logging

Anchorage is Alaska's largest city.

businesses. Many newcomers work in these trades. Others start their own businesses or settle in Alaska's bush.

European Backgrounds
About 75 percent of Alaskans have European backgrounds. Russians were Alaska's first European settlers. They came to the region that is now Alaska in the 1700s. They started Alaska's fur trade. They built Russian Orthodox churches.

In the 1800s, more settlers with European backgrounds came from Canada and the Lower 48. Alaskans call the U.S. mainland the Lower 48. Others came directly from European countries. Early settlers started Alaska's fishing, mining, and logging businesses.

Today, many Alaskans have English, German, and Irish ancestors. Some Alaskans have Russian backgrounds. Most of these Russian people have arrived in recent years.

Native Americans
Alaska's Native Americans include Eskimos, Aleuts, and Athabascans. They also include Haidas, Tlingits, and Tsimshians. These groups make up about 16 percent of Alaska's population.

Alaska has the largest population of Eskimos and Aleuts among the states. About 44,000 Eskimos live there. The Inupiat live mainly in the north. The Yupik live in southwestern Alaska. Many Eskimos fish or raise reindeer for a living.

About 10,000 Aleuts live in Alaska. The Aleuts live on the Aleutian Islands and the Alaska Peninsula.

About 32,000 other Native Americans live in Alaska. Athabascans live in central Alaska. Haidas, Tlingits, and Tsimshians live in the southeast.

African Americans

In 1870, only six African Americans lived in Alaska. Today, about four percent of Alaska's population is African American.

Some African Americans work on U.S. military bases. Others work on fishing boats or in businesses.

Asian Americans and Hispanic Americans

Recently, Alaska's Asian and Hispanic populations have doubled. About 20,000 Asian Americans live in Alaska. Most came from Korea and the Philippines. About 18,000 Hispanics live in Alaska. Most Hispanics came from Mexico.

Chapter 4
Alaska History

Long ago, a land bridge connected Russia to the land that is now Alaska. Many people entered the Alaska area over the land bridge. They were early relatives of Athabascan, Tlingit, and Haida people. About 14,000 years ago, the Bering Sea covered the land bridge. Eskimos and Aleuts entered Alaska by boat about 9,000 years ago.

Russian Alaska

In 1741, people exploring for Russia sailed to Alaska's Kayak Island. They brought sea otter furs back to Russia.

In 1743, Russian fur traders arrived in the Aleutian Islands. The islands are the tops of underwater mountains. By 1784, a Russian trading post stood on Kodiak Island. But few Russian families settled in Alaska.

Athabascan and Tlingit people entered the Alaska area over a land bridge. Today they honor their relatives' way of life through dances.

Americans Gain Control

By the 1860s, Russia had lost interest in Alaska. Fur trading had slowed. Few sea otters were left in Alaska.

In the mid-1800s, American fishing and mining companies wanted to move into Alaska. In 1867, the United States bought the Alaska territory. Russia sold Alaska for $7.2 million.

Salmon canneries opened in Sitka and Klawock in 1878. A few saw mills also opened in southeastern Alaska.

At first, few Americans moved to the Alaskan Territory. Most Americans thought of the territory as a faraway, frozen land.

The Gold Rush

In 1880, Joe Juneau and Dick Harris discovered gold. The two men founded the town of Juneau near their gold strike. The town grew quickly. In 1896, gold was found in the Yukon area of Canada. Thousands of miners rushed through Alaska to the goldfields there. These miners later followed more gold rushes into Alaska.

In 1898, people found gold in Nome. In 1902, gold mining started in Fairbanks. By 1910, about

64,000 people lived in Alaska. Alaska's population had almost doubled since 1880.

The Early Alaska Territory
In 1912, the U.S. Congress created the Alaska Territory. Alaskans named Juneau the territory's capital. They elected a territorial legislature. A legislature is a group of people that make laws. The legislature met in Juneau.

Alaska kept growing. Coal and copper mines opened. A telegraph connected Alaska with the

Workers in Alaska have canned salmon since 1878.

Lower 48. By 1923, a railroad ran from Seward to Fairbanks.

The Great Depression
In 1929, the Great Depression (1929-1939) affected the entire nation. Alaska's copper mines closed. Saw mills closed. Many Alaskans lost their jobs.

In 1933, the U.S. government started the New Deal. The New Deal program provided jobs for many people in the United States. Alaskans built harbors and roads. The government also moved 200 families to live and farm in the Matanuska Valley. These families came from the Lower 48.

World War II
In 1941, Japan attacked the U.S. Navy base at Pearl Harbor, Hawaii. This attack brought the United States into World War II (1939-1945).

Japanese forces captured the Aleutian Islands of Attu and Kiska in 1942. In 1943, U.S. troops recaptured Attu and Kiska islands. This was the only fighting on U.S. land during the war.

The war brought growth to Alaska. In 1942, the U.S. government built the Alaska Highway

The U.S. government moved 200 families to live and farm in the Matanuska Valley.

through Canada. It joined Alaska with the Lower 48. The government also built army and air force bases in Alaska. The military stationed thousands of soldiers there.

Statehood and Oil

In 1959, the U.S. Congress made Alaska the 49th state. Juneau remained the state capital.

In 1968, people found oil in Prudhoe Bay. Workers came to build the Trans-Alaska Pipeline.

This pipeline carries oil 800 miles (1,288 kilometers) from Prudhoe Bay to Valdez in Alaska. It was finished in 1977.

Alaska's government earns billions of dollars from oil. Every year, each Alaskan receives about $1,000 from the state government. This amount is each Alaskan's share of the oil money.

The Trans-Alaska Pipeline carries oil from Prudhoe Bay to Valdez.

Decisions about Land Use

The U.S. government and the state of Alaska own most of Alaska's land. In 1971, the U.S. government returned 40 million acres (18 million hectares) of land to Alaska's Native Americans.

Most of the remaining government land is national parkland, forests, and wildlife refuges. By the 1990s, some Alaskans wanted to drill for the oil that lies under the Arctic Wildlife Refuge.

Some Alaskans want to allow more logging in the Tongass National Forest. This is a rain forest. Huge red cedars and Sitka spruce grow in the forest.

Other Alaskans want these lands to remain wilderness. They hope Alaska will continue to be North America's last frontier. A frontier is an undeveloped and unexplored area. Alaska is one of the few places left in North America that has large areas of undeveloped land.

Chapter 5
Alaska Business

Mining is Alaska's most important business. Fishing and logging are also important. Government, trade, and tourism are major service businesses. Farming and manufacturing are small businesses in Alaska.

Mining

Mining brings in 32 percent of Alaska's income. No other state receives as much of its income from mining.

Mining makes up about 85 percent of the income for state government. Most of Alaska's mining income comes from oil. Prudhoe Bay has one of the world's largest oil fields. People in Fairbanks and Nome still mine gold. Kotzebue has the nation's largest zinc mine.

Most of Alaska's mining income comes from oil.

Fishing

Alaska has the nation's most profitable fish catch. Each year, the catch is worth about $2 billion. People mainly catch salmon, crabs, and cod.

Agriculture

Alaska's largest farming area is the Matanuska Valley. In the summer, its temperatures are warm. The sun shines about 20 hours a day. The long daylight hours help cabbages grow as big as 90 pounds (41 kilograms). Large carrots and turnips also grow well there.

Dairy cattle are important farm animals. Milk from the cattle is Alaska's most valuable agricultural product.

Manufacturing

Alaska makes few manufactured goods. Processed fish is the leading manufactured product. Wood and paper products are also important. Mills use wood from trees in Alaska's southeastern rain forest to make these

Alaska has the nation's most profitable fish catch.

products. Most wood products are shipped
to Japan.

Alaskan manufacturers make machinery and
computer equipment. Manufacturers also make
construction goods and handcrafted products.

Services Industries

Many people in Alaska work for the United
States government. Most government workers
in Alaska have jobs on military bases. Others
work in Alaska's national parks and forests.
Many other men and women work for state and
city governments.

Anchorage, Dutch Harbor, and Valdez are
major trading ports. Companies ship most of
Alaska's fish products and oil from these ports.

Goods also arrive in ships that dock at
Alaska's major ports. Alaskans must ship in
goods from other countries and the Lower 48.
Many of these goods come from Japan and
Canada. Alaskans do not grow enough food for
themselves. They do not make enough
manufactured products either.

Mills use wood from trees in Alaska's southeastern rain forest to make wood and paper products.

More than 1 million tourists visit Alaska each year. They spend more than $800 million. Owners of Alaska's resorts and wilderness camps make much of this money. Many people also take cruises along Alaska's southeastern coast.

Chapter 6

Seeing the Sights

Alaska has 15 national parks and 16 wildlife refuges. These areas offer many outdoor adventures. Visitors learn about the state's history in Alaska's cities and towns.

The Panhandle

Juneau is in southeast Alaska. This is the state capital. Mendenhall Glacier lies 15 miles from the city. Visitors can walk onto this huge ice field.

Sitka was once the Russian capital of Alaska. Some buildings built by Russians still stand there. The Sheldon Jackson Museum exhibits arts and crafts of Alaska's Native Americans.

Glacier Bay National Park is northwest of Juneau. Most of the park's visitors travel there on cruise ships.

People call southeastern Alaska the Panhandle. A panhandle is a narrow area of land that sticks

Juneau is Alaska's capital city.

out from a larger area of land. On a map it looks like the handle of a frying pan.

The Inside Passage is a waterway that winds through the Panhandle. Cruise ships and ferries use this waterway. They carry people between the cities of the Panhandle.

Ketchikan is at the Panhandle's southern tip. The world's largest totem pole collection is at The Totem Heritage Center there.

Southcentral Alaska

Anchorage lies on Cook Inlet. The Anchorage Museum of History and Art exhibits Alaskan art and village life.

The Alaska Aviation Heritage Museum is outside Anchorage. Visitors learn about Alaska's bush planes and seaplanes. Seaplanes are planes that can take off from and land on water.

Wrangell-St. Elias National Park is the nation's largest national park. Visitors can see two of the state's largest glaciers.

Kenai Fjords National Park is on the Kenai Peninsula. A fjord is a long, narrow inlet of ocean between high cliffs. Visitors on cruise ships see glacier-covered mountains that rise from the Gulf of Alaska.

Southwestern Alaska

Kodiak National Wildlife Refuge covers two-thirds of Kodiak Island. Large Kodiak brown bears live there.

Novarupta Volcano is in Katmai National Park. A desert of ash formed on the Alaska Peninsula when the volcano erupted in 1912.

Bethel is Alaska's largest city in the bush. It sits in the middle of the Yukon Delta National Wildlife Refuge. This is the nation's largest wildlife refuge. Geese, swans, and ducks nest in the refuge.

The Inside Passage is a waterway that winds through the Panhandle. Cruise ships and ferries use this waterway.

Northern Alaska

Nome is on the Seward Peninsula. Visitors there can learn how to pan for gold. They can keep any gold they find.

Kotzebue is the oldest Inupiat village. The Museum of the Arctic in Kotzebue holds many demonstrations. A demonstration is a performance to show how something is done. One demonstration is the blanket toss. A group of people hold a walrus skin blanket. They toss a person standing on the blanket into the air.

Two national parks are in the Brooks Mountain Range. They are Kobuk Valley and Gates of the Arctic National Parks. The Arctic National Wildlife Refuge lies farther east.

Barrow is the nation's northernmost town. Many Inupiat live there. Visitors shop for masks and dolls made by the Inupiat.

Interior Alaska

Fort Yukon is the state's largest Athabascan village. Athabascan women are famous for their beautiful beadwork.

Fairbanks is home to the University of Alaska. Scientists there study the northern lights. The northern lights is a colorful light display that appears in the northern night sky.

Mount McKinley stands in the middle of Denali National Park. Some Alaskans call it Mount Denali. Denali means the High One in the Athabascan language. Hikers and campers explore the park's meadows and lakes. Mountain climbers try to reach Mount McKinley's highest peak.

Alaska Time Line

48,000 B.C.-18,000 B.C.—Athabascans, Tlingits, and Haidas enter the Alaska area by crossing the Bering Land Bridge from Russia.

7000-4000 B.C.—Eskimos and Aleuts cross the Bering Sea and enter Alaska.

1741—Danish explorer Vitus Bering explores Kayak Island for Russia.

1743—Russian hunters and fur traders arrive on the Aleutian Islands.

1770s—Spanish and British explorers reach Alaska.

1784—Russians build their first permanent settlement on Kodiak Island.

1807—Sitka becomes the capital of Russian America.

1867—The United States purchases the land that is now Alaska from Russia for $7.2 million.

1880—Joe Juneau and Dick Harris find gold near present-day Juneau.

1896—Gold is discovered in the Klondike area of Canada. Thousands of miners come through Alaska to reach the goldfields.

1898—Miners discover gold in Nome.

1902—Miners discover gold near Fairbanks.

1910—Builders complete the Iditarod Trail between Knik and Nome.

1912—The U.S. Congress creates the Alaskan Territory.

1914—Settlers found Anchorage.

1935—The U.S. government sends 200 families to live and farm in the Matanuska Valley.

1942-1943—Japan invades the Aleutian Islands of Attu and Kiska; U.S. forces regain the islands.

1959—Alaska becomes the 49th state.

1964—The largest earthquake in North American history hits Anchorage, killing 131 people.

1968—People find oil at Prudhoe Bay.

1971—The United States government gives Alaska's native people 40 million acres (18 million hectares) of land and $962.5 million.

1973—Mushers race in the first Iditarod Trail Sled Dog Race.

1977—Workers complete the Trans-Alaska Pipeline from Prudhoe Bay to Valdez.

1996—The U.S. government allows logging in the Tongass National Forest and lifts the ban on shipping oil from Prudhoe Bay to other countries.

Famous Alaskans

Aleksandr Andreyevich Baranov (1746-1819) Russian fur trader who became the first governor of Russian America and founded present-day Sitka (1799).

Susan Butcher (1954-) With Joe Redington, drove the first sled dog team to the top of Mount McKinley (1978); lives in Manley.

Nora M. Dauenhauer (1927-) Tlingit writer who works to preserve Tlingit stories and has written spelling and grammar books in the Tlingit language; born in Juneau.

Carl Ben Eielson (1897-1929) Pioneer bush pilot; made first Alaska air mail flight in 1924.

Taras Genet (1978-) At age 12, became the youngest person to reach Mount McKinley's summit (1991); born in Denali National Park.

Walter Harper (1893?-1915?) Athabascan who became the first person to reach the summit of Mount McKinley (1913); born in Nenana.

Elizabeth Wannamaker Peratrovich (1911-1958) Former president of the Alaska Native Sisterhood whose work led to Alaska's Equal Rights Law (1945); born in Sitka.

Joe Redington Sr. (1917-) Organized the Iditarod Trail Sled Dog Race (1973) and has taken part in eight races, including the 1997 race; has lived in Knik since 1948.

Libby Riddles (1956-) First woman to win the Iditarod Trail Sled Dog Race (1985); her books *Race Across Alaska* and *Storm Run* are about the Iditarod; lives in Wasilla.

Leonhard Seppala (1877-1966) Famed dog sled racer who helped prevent a diptheria epidemic by mushing medicine to Nome in 1925.

Hudson Stuck (1863-1920) Missionary and mountain climber; worked with the Athabascan people and tried to preserve their way of life; led the first group to reach the peak of Mount McKinley (1913).

Words to Know

bush (BUSH)—wilderness areas with few roads

epidemic (ep-uh-DEM-ik)—the rapid spread of an illness through a population

fjord (FYORD)—a long, narrow inlet of ocean between high cliffs

glacier (GLAY-shur)—a huge sheet of slowly moving ice

Inside Passage (IN-side PASS-ij)—a waterway that winds through Alaska's Panhandle

mush (MUHSH)—to travel using a sled dog team

musher (MUHSH-ur)—the driver of a sled dog team

muskeg (MUHSS-keg)—soft, wet land

panhandle (PAN-han-duhl)—a narrow area of land that sticks out from a larger area of land

seaplane (SEE-plane)—a plane that can take off from and land on water

tundra (TUHN-druh)—treeless land where the ground below surface is always frozen

To Learn More

Ferrell, Nancy Warren. *Alaska: A Land in Motion*. Fairbanks: University of Alaska, 1994.

Fradin, Dennis Brindell. *Alaska*. From Sea to Shining Sea. Chicago: Children's Press, 1993.

Petersen, David. *Denali National Park and Preserve*. Danbury, Conn.: Children's Press, 1996.

Ragan, John David. *The Explorers of Alaska*. New York: Chelsea House, 1992.

Internet Sites

City.net Alaska
http://www.city.net/countries/united_states/alaska/
State of Alaska
http://www.state.ak.us/
Travel.org Alaska
http://travel.org/alaska.html

Useful Addresses

Alaska Department of Fish and Game
211 Mission Road
Kodiak, AK 99615

Denali National Park and Preserve
National Park Service
P.O. Box 9
Denali Park, AK 99755

Iditarod Trail Sled Dog Race Headquarters
P.O. Box 870800
Wasilla, AK 99687

Kikiktagruk Inupiat Corporation
P.O. Box 1050
Kotzebue, AK 99752

Mendenhall Glacier
U.S. Forest Service
Tongass National Forest, Juneau Ranger District
8465 Old Dairy Road
Juneau, AK 99801

Caribou live in Alaska's wilderness areas.

Index